DISC

Discovering

DUCKS, GEESE AND SWANS

Anthony Wharton

Artwork by Jackie Harland

The Bookwright Press
New York · 1987

Discovering Nature

Discovering Ants
Discovering Bees and Wasps
Discovering Beetles
Discovering Birds of Prey
Discovering Butterflies and Moths
Discovering Crabs and Lobsters
Discovering Crickets and Grasshoppers
Discovering Ducks, Geese and Swans
Discovering Flies

Discovering Flowering Plants
Discovering Frogs and Toads
Discovering Rabbits and Hares
Discovering Rats and Mice
Discovering Sea birds
Discovering Slugs and Snails
Discovering Snakes and Lizards
Discovering Spiders
Discovering Squirrels
Discovering Worms

Further titles are in preparation

Editor: Joan Walters

First published in the
United States in 1987 by
The Bookwright Press
387 Park Avenue South
New York, NY 10016

First published in 1987 by
Wayland (Publishers) Limited
61 Western Road, Hove
East Sussex BN3 1JD, England

ISBN 0–531–18126–X

Library of Congress Catalog Card Number: 86–72825

Typeset by DP Press Ltd., Sevenoaks, Kent
Printed in Italy by Sagdos S.p.A., Milan

Cover A pair of Canada geese and their goslings.

Frontispiece   An eider duck on her nest hidden in vegetation.

Contents

1
Introducing Ducks, Geese and Swans

Almost all wildfowl have broad, flat bills. This is a lesser scaup.

The Wildfowl Family

Ducks, geese and swans make up a family of birds usually called wildfowl, although they are not fowls like chickens or turkeys. They have developed from land birds that have learned to swim, and now live, feed and **breed** on or near water. For this reason, they are sometimes called waterfowl. Some prefer the sea, while others have chosen rivers, lakes, ponds or marshes for their homes. Many wildfowl fly, feed and rest in **flocks**.

All of them have special features, such as webbed feet and broad, flat bills, or beaks, to help them make the most of their watery **habitat**. There are about 150 different kinds of wildfowl and many differences in the way they look and behave.

Most ducks, geese and swans fly well and many **migrate** from one part of the world to another at different times of the year. Some, such as the mallard duck and the mute swan, have **adapted** to many different kinds of habitat, so they can be found in several parts of the world. Others, like the ne-ne ("nay-nay"), or Hawaiian goose, and the Australian black swan, are found in only a few places. A few kinds of wildfowl, like the flightless steamer duck from the Falkland Islands, have settled on remote islands and have slowly changed to suit the conditions found there. They have therefore lost the **instinct** to migrate and several have even lost the power of flight completely.

Wildfowl can often be seen in flocks, especially in winter. These are on a park pool in the middle of a town.

Tribes of Wildfowl

Scientists have arranged wildfowl into ten groups called tribes. Each one is made up of a number of different kinds of birds with similar features or that behave in a similar way.

All the geese and the eight kinds of swans have been put into a single tribe. One reason for this is that a male swan, or cob, looks very much like the female, or pen, and a male goose, or gander, closely resembles the female. Geese and swans also keep the same mate for life.

The other tribes are made up only of ducks, although several kinds have the word "geese" in their names. Sheldgeese and pygmy geese are two examples that have been grouped with the ducks because they are not true geese.

Most male and female ducks look different from each other for much of the year and they do not normally pair for life. Even so, they have not all been put into one tribe, as the different kinds vary so much in appearance and behavior. For example, those ducks that feed at the surface of the water are called dabbling ducks. They make up the largest and most widely spread tribe of all.

Mallards are members of the dabbling ducks tribe. The male's plumage is brighter than that of his mate for most of the year.

The odd looking spur-winged goose from Africa is not a true goose. It is included in the tribe of wood or perching ducks.

There are several tribes of diving ducks, which find their food by swimming underwater. Of these, two

Like all true geese, male and female white-fronted geese look very much alike.

are found only at sea. Stiff-tails, wood or perching ducks and torrent ducks are some of the other strange names given to tribes of ducks.

2
What are Wildfowl?

Most ducks are shaped like this Philippine duck with its stout body and short neck and legs.

Taking a Close Look

Most wildfowl have stout bodies, flattened underneath, and narrow, pointed wings. They all have longish necks, although ducks generally have shorter necks than either geese or swans.

Wildfowl usually have fairly short legs, each foot having three large, webbed toes at the front and a small hind-toe. Their legs are toward the rear of the body, which means that their feet make good paddles for swimming. However, it also means that, when on land, they waddle rather than walk. Geese, which graze a lot on land, have their feet farther forward than ducks and swans and so walk less clumsily.

Many wildfowl, especially dabbling ducks, have rather broad, flat bills that are rounded at the tip. A few, such as the fish-eating sawbill ducks, have longer, more pointed bills, while others have a slight hook at the end of the bill. Several kinds of wildfowl have a comb or knob above the bill, and others, such as the tufted duck and the colorful mandarin, have a crest or tuft of feathers at the back of the head.

Ducks, geese and swans keep their feathers well oiled to prevent them from becoming waterlogged. Beneath their top feathers they have a layer of soft **down** to keep out the cold. Geese and swans change their body feathers only once a year, whereas most ducks **molt** twice yearly.

THE PARTS OF A MALLARD DRAKE

bill

wing

breast

tail feathers

speculum

three webbed toes

hind toe

The Biggest and the Smallest

Swans are the largest and most graceful of the wildfowl. A fully grown trumpeter swan, the largest kind of swan, may measure more than

A fully grown male swan is a large bird with powerful wings.

1.5 m (5 ft) from the bill-tip to the tip of the tail. It can reach a weight of 20 kg (44 lb). Its wings, when fully spread, can measure over 2 m (6.5 ft) from wing-tip to wing-tip. A blow from an adult swan's wing can be quite painful and knock a person over. In contrast the smallest swan, the coscoroba swan from South America, is only the size of a small goose.

Geese are usually smaller than swans, but they are still quite large. An adult Canada goose, one of the largest kinds of geese, is about 1 m (3.28 ft) long and 8 kg (17.6 lb) in weight.

Ducks vary a great deal in size, but are nearly always much smaller than either geese or swans. A mallard, the largest and commonest dabbling duck, is about 55 cm (22 in) long, although a number of ducks from other tribes are larger. Some of the smallest are teals, which may be only 30 cm (12 in) long, or even less.

The little tufted duck, which can be seen in many parts of the world, is only about 17 inches long.

Above *This colorful band of wing feathers is the speculum of a Baikal teal.*

Below *Bewick and whooper swans have similar, but not identical, bills. Each bird can be recognized by its bill pattern.*

Colors and Patterns

Most adult swans are white, although there is one black swan and another kind has a black head and neck. You can learn to identify the different kinds of white swans by the color of their bills. Baby swans, or cygnets, are brownish gray and do not have colorful bills like their parents.

Geese vary more than swans in color and pattern, but few are brightly colored. They may be white, gray, or white, black and brown. The most colorful kind of goose is probably the red-breasted goose, but the "red" is really a sort of brown.

It is best to identify the different kinds of geese by looking at the color and pattern together. The Canada goose, for example, is mostly brown, but has light underparts and a black neck and head with a white chin. Baby geese, or goslings, are usually dirty yellow in color.

Ducks, especially the **drakes**, vary in color and pattern even more than geese. Many drakes are very colorful indeed. For a short time each year, however, they lose their bright breeding **plumage** and replace it with more drab plumage like that of the females.

Most ducks have a patch of colorful wing feathers called a **speculum**. This probably helps them identify other ducks of the same kind. Ducklings are mostly yellow or dingy brown, usually with a few darker markings.

The names of wildfowl often describe their color. This is a female ruddy shelduck, which has rust-colored plumage.

The Noises Wildfowl Make

The sounds that wildfowl make differ according to the kind of wildfowl they are and the tribe to which they belong. Some are very noisy indeed, while others are mostly silent or have very soft calls.

Most of the time swans are not noisy birds, but trumpeter, whistling, whooper and Bewick's swans sometimes make trumpeting or bugling noises. The mute swan, its name means "silent," hisses when it is angry. Geese usually "honk," although, like swans, they hiss when they defend their nests or young.

For centuries people thought that swans sang a very tuneful song just before they died. We know now that this is not true; however, we still use the expression "swan song" to describe what someone does toward the end of life.

This black swan is hissing at someone who has approached its nest.

The white-faced tree duck belongs to a tribe called whistling ducks.

Geese in flight are often heard "honking" before they come into sight.

Just as the colors of ducks vary a great deal, so the sounds they make differ a lot too. The drakes of many kinds of dabbling ducks, especially in the northern **hemisphere**, have distinctive, often quite tuneful calls.

The females mainly have "quacking" calls, like most, but not all other ducks. Whistling ducks get their name from the shrill whistling noises they make. Other wildfowl "bark," "cluck," "rattle," "grunt" or even "laugh."

3
Food and Feeding

The whooper swan, like all birds, needs to drink regularly.

How Wildfowl Feed

Wildfowl find most of their food in or near water. Their feeding habits are quite varied, but mainly involve dabbling, diving or grazing. Their bills are specially adapted to the way they feed and to the different kinds of food they eat.

There are rows of fine notches along the edges of their bills. These are called *lamellae.* They form the "saw" of the sawbill ducks, and help them grip the fish they catch. Dabbling ducks use their *lamellae* to filter food from the surface of the water or from just beneath it. Swans, geese and a few kinds of ducks use them to nip off grass and other plants when they are grazing on land. Geese in particular like to flock to fields to graze on farm crops. Many kinds of wildfowl feed in flocks, as they find food more easily this way.

This eider duck is using its feet to disturb the mud in its search for food.

The lamellae *can be clearly seen on the bill of this white-fronted goose.*

Some wildfowl, especially dabbling ducks and swans, find food in mud at the bottom of shallow water. To do this dabbling ducks up-end themselves and seem to stand on their heads. Swans can often be seen using their long, flexible necks to reach plant food beneath the surface. Ducklings, goslings and cygnets can see and swim as soon as they hatch and can find food when they are only a day old. Most are able to dive for food, even when their parents do not normally dive at all.

What Wildfowl Eat

Plant material forms the basic food of many kinds of wildfowl, particularly of geese and swans. Geese love to nibble grass, young cereal crops and grain. They will even eat potatoes. Swans seem to prefer to feed on underwater plants, which they find just beneath the surface.

Dabbling ducks eat lots of tiny seeds, as well as small pieces of waterweed. They also eat small insects and water snails. Baby dabbling ducks feed almost entirely on insects

Barnacle geese grazing at the edge of a pond. Grass forms part of the diet of many geese.

until they are about three weeks old.

Diving ducks eat more animal food than dabblers. In fresh water many diving ducks feed on small shellfish and insects from the mud on the bottom, but ducks such as pochards and scaup like the roots and tubers of underwater plants.

In the sea the sawbill ducks feed mainly on small fish and **plankton**, while other sea ducks, like scoters and eiders, eat a lot of shellfish, which they swallow whole.

Wildfowl are often poisoned by swallowing fishermen's lead weights, which they mistake for grit or seed.

Wildfowl eat grit to help them break down and digest their food. In some parts of the world many wildfowl have died in recent years through swallowing lead shotgun pellets or the weights that fishermen use on their lines. The birds mistake them for grit or seeds and die from lead poisoning.

4
Courting and Mating

Mute swans usually pair for life.

Finding a Mate

Like humans, wildfowl have only one **mate** at a time, although many kinds of ducks change partners each year. Whether or not they pair for life, both males and females choose their mates with great care. This usually involves a sort of showing off called **courting**, which often takes place before the breeding season starts.

The male ducks, or drakes, in their colorful breeding plumage, do much of the courting. Their behavior includes many different and amusing displays, such as "head-shaking," "bill-dipping," "neck-stretching" and "tail-flicking."

Courtship is often carried out in small flocks and is usually quite a noisy affair. A female shows she is ready to accept a mate by responding to a male's behavior with a display of her own, although this is usually less

COURTING DISPLAYS

male ruddy duck blowing bubbles

male pochard head-shaking

striking than that of the male.

When both sexes of a kind of wildfowl look alike, the female often shows off as much as the male. Displays of this sort can help to strengthen partnerships already made. In this case the displays are known as "pair-bonding."

Geese and swans do not usually mate until they are four or five years old, but ducks may breed at just one year old.

The colorful breeding plumage of a mallard drake helps him attract a mate.

Nests and Eggs

Spring is the time when wildfowl of the northern hemisphere build their nests. Waterfowl that live in tropical regions usually have a longer breeding season. The area around the nest of each pair of birds is called a territory. It is defended bravely against intruders. The territories of wildfowl that nest in **colonies** are usually small. Those kinds of wildfowl that nest away from other birds tend to

A Canada goose on her nest, which she has built among brambles and bluebells.

The nest of an eider duck lined with soft down from her breast to cushion the eggs.

have larger territories.

Each kind of duck, goose and swan has a favorite type of nesting place. This may be on the bank of a river or lake, on an island, among reeds, in a marsh, on the seashore, in a suitable hole in the ground, or even in a hole in a tree.

Both male and female swans help with nest building. The nest is large and made mainly of plant material. It

A mute swan and her cygnet. Swans build bulky nests out of plant material in very open places.

is usually very easy to see. Goose and duck nests are built by the female only and are more likely to be well hidden among **vegetation**. Sticks, grass and other plants are the main materials used for building, but the nest is usually lined with down from the female's breast. This keeps the eggs warm, dry and hidden when the female leaves the nest.

Wildfowl eggs are pale in color and have no markings. They are oval in shape rather than pointed at one end. Some lay as few as two eggs. Others may lay twenty or more. Swan eggs can weigh over 350 g (12 oz), while those of very small ducks may weigh 30 g (1 oz) or less.

Parents and Young

When the eggs have all been laid they have to be **incubated**. This takes between twenty-two and thirty-nine days, depending mainly on the size of the bird. Usually only the female incubates, but some kinds of wildfowl share the work. If the male does not help, he may stand guard at the nest

Young cygnets, like those of this black-necked swan from South Africa, often take a ride on a parent's back.

Right *Young ducklings, even those of white domesticated ducks, are always yellow, brown, or yellow and brown together. They usually stay close to their parents when they are very small.*

or leave his mate altogether.

When the eggs hatch, the baby birds quickly become attached to the first living creature they see and hear. This is usually a parent, but young wildfowl have been known to **imprint** on other birds or even on people.

The young soon leave the nest. They are often able to tumble straight into the water, even from a nest in a tree. They quickly learn to follow their parents to look for food.

Both parents of some kinds of wildfowl care for their babies, while with other kinds only the mother does so. The baby birds usually snuggle together underneath a parent when they need to sleep. Some even climb on to their parents' backs to rest or to be carried around.

Young geese and swans stay with their parents for almost a year and may fly with them when they migrate. Ducks usually care for their ducklings only until they have **fledged**.

5
Migration

A pink-footed goose, which has flown south from the Arctic to spend the winter in Britain, where it is less cold. It often has to find food under the snow.

Why Wildfowl Migrate

Just like some other families of birds, many wildfowl find life easier if they fly from one region of the world to another at different times of the year. This is called migration. People have been fascinated by it since ancient times, because of the long distances that some birds travel. Migrating wildfowl may fly distances as great as 4,000 km (2,500 mi).

Most wildfowl that migrate live in the northern hemisphere. Many kinds, particularly geese and swans, breed in the Arctic **tundra**, where the ground may be free of snow for only two or three months of the year. Although the summer there is very short, the hours of daylight are long. The birds benefit from the extra hours of daylight, because they have more time to feed on the rich food supplies found there in summer.

Snow geese, like many other wildfowl, fly great distances when they migrate for the summer to their breeding grounds.

There is also plenty of living space and fewer **predators** to kill the newly hatched young birds.

However, conditions quickly become too hard for the birds once the summer is over. They therefore fly south to spend the winter in areas where it is less cold and where they can find food more easily.

Many kinds of wildfowl in Australia migrate according to the weather. There are huge areas of desert in Australia and drought is common. The birds do not follow a regular route at the same time each year, but follow the rains to areas where there is plenty of food and water.

Above *Flocks of wildfowl are often very large indeed. These are barnacle geese.*

Below *A numbered band on the leg of a pink-footed goose. Banding helps scientists to track a bird's movements.*

How Wildfowl Migrate

How migrating wildfowl find their way has puzzled people for hundreds of years, for they seem to know exactly where they are going. Many of them return to the same place year after year.

Some young birds no doubt learn from their parents, but it is equally certain that others find their way on their own. They probably use the positions of the sun and stars to help them **navigate**. A cloudy sky sometimes causes them to lose their way and windy weather blows them off course. Many people believe that the earth's **magnetism** may help to guide the migrating birds.

Much work is being done to find out more about the travels of migrating birds. Banding provides a lot of new information. Small, numbered bands are placed on the

legs of captured birds, which are then released. Many of these bands are recovered when the birds are caught or found dead elsewhere. This helps scientists to track the birds' movements. **Radar** is also used to track the movements of migrating birds.

Wildfowl usually migrate in flocks. Although many travel at night, they can sometimes be seen flying

Bar-headed geese on migration have been seen flying over the top of Mount Everest.

overhead in a V-formation in the spring and autumn.

Most migrating wildfowl fly quite quickly. Some ducks reach a speed of almost 100 kph (62 mph). The height at which wildfowl migrate varies a lot, but geese have been seen flying at a height of over 9,000 m (29,000 ft).

6
Wildfowl and People

These are the kind of common white duck you might see on a farm.

Domestic Wildfowl

Some of the earliest birds to be **domesticated** were geese. The greylag goose of Europe and Asia is the ancestor of most present-day farmyard geese. Two other kinds of domestic geese, the Chinese and the African, are both descended from the swan goose of Eastern Asia.

The Romans enjoyed eating goose liver and fattened up geese specially. Even today, in France, geese are fed a special diet to fatten their livers, which are used to make a delicacy called *pâté de foie gras*. In medieval Britain goose fairs were held, where thousands of geese were bought and sold.

Ducks were first domesticated in China more than 2,000 years ago. Five kinds of common farmyard ducks have developed from the mallard. They are the white

Aylesbury and Pekin ducks and the darker Rouen ducks, which are all reared for meat, and khaki campbells and runner ducks, which are good egg-layers.

Eiderdown bed covers are often filled with real down from eider ducks. In Iceland many thousands of eiders are farmed for their down. The feathers and down of other ducks, and geese, are also used to stuff pillows and quilts.

Greylag geese were the ancestors of most domesticated geese.

Mute swans have been partly domesticated in Europe since the Middle Ages. In Britain they once provided a tasty delicacy for royalty, to whom they mainly belonged. Even today swans on the Thames River are counted and the young ones **pinioned** each year. Their bills are also marked during a ceremony called "swan-upping."

People as Enemies

People and their activities are the direct cause of many of the dangers faced by wildfowl. For centuries ducks and geese have been trapped for food in one way or another.

Decoys have been used for hundreds of years to trap wildfowl for food. A decoy is a pond with several net-covered tunnels leading from it. Wild ducks were tempted down onto the pond by tame white ducks called "call-ducks," and then chased along the tunnels by a dog. One or two decoys are still in use to catch ducks for banding. The word "decoy" is also used to describe a painted, floating model of a duck, used to attract wild birds within shooting range.

Being hunted with shotguns is one of the greatest dangers faced by ducks, geese and swans. Once this was mainly to obtain food, but sport has been the main aim in recent years.

Oil, spilled or discharged from tankers, can also cause deaths among wildfowl, especially sea ducks such as scoters and eiders. Birds that are covered with oil soon die because they are unable to swim or fly.

Pesticides, used to control pests and diseases of grain crops, have poisoned many grazing geese.

Model painted ducks, called decoys, are used to attract wild ducks within shooting range. These represent a pochard drake on the left, and a pair of mallards.

Wildfowl are also sometimes killed by flying into overhead power lines or even by crashing into aircraft.

Part of one of the tubes or "horns" of a trap used for catching wildfowl. This one is now only used to catch birds for banding.

Protecting Wildfowl

It is very important for us to protect all forms of wildlife. This protection is called conservation. Although many kinds of wildfowl are still very common, most benefit from some help and protection against the

In England, the Wildfowl Trust supports this reserve where many kinds of ducks, geese and swans can live and breed in peace.

dangers that face them.

One way of providing this protection is by setting up places where wildfowl can live and breed in peace. As long ago as A.D. 700, Saint Cuthbert, who lived on the Farne Islands, off the northeast coast of England, realized the need for conservation and gave protection to eider ducks.

Nowadays, there are many more people who care about wildlife and try to protect it. Conservation groups have saved rare birds, such as the Hawaiian goose and the white-winged wood duck, from becoming **extinct** by breeding them in captivity.

Since the middle of the last century many laws have been passed to protect wild birds. Despite such measures, many birds, including four kinds of wildfowl, have become extinct.

You may be able to do something to help protect wildlife yourself in a small way, perhaps by joining a conservation group such as the Audubon Society. You can certainly help by trying not to disturb nesting birds when you are out watching wildfowl. For example, if you have a dog, leave it at home. Dogs can cause great damage if they are allowed to wander freely where wildfowl are feeding and nesting.

The ne-ne, or Hawaiian goose, that was saved from probable extinction by being bred at a wildfowl reserve in England.

7
Watching Wildfowl

Lots of different kinds of wildfowl can usually be seen at wildfowl reserves.

Where to See Wildfowl

Most people live within easy reach of places where wildfowl can be seen. Even if you live in a town or city, you probably have a park nearby with a pond or lake where you can watch some of the common ducks, geese and swans. These may be wild birds, such as mallards, Canada geese and mute swans, or they may be more unusual kinds of "ornamental" wildfowl, brought from distant parts of the world, such as the mandarin duck from China and Japan.

You may be very lucky and live near a lake or river, or even by the ocean, where flocks of less common wildfowl can often be seen. For example, Brant geese and snow geese breed during the summer in the Arctic tundra, but they all move south for the winter. Brant geese can be seen wintering on the east and west coasts of the United

States. Snow geese can be found in the western states. You will soon learn the best places to see wildfowl near your home if you talk to other bird-watchers. Your local library may also provide you with useful information.

Nowadays there are many nature reserves and **refuges** where you can study wildfowl at close range. These reserves have large collections of

Many families visit wildfowl reserves each year and are able to watch and even feed the birds at very close range.

wildfowl from all over the world, as well as visiting flocks of wild birds. Such places often have special information centers to provide you with interesting facts about the birds to be found there.

How to Watch

You will probably want to find out the names of the wildfowl you see. For this you need a field guide. A field guide is a book with pictures and descriptions of the birds you are likely to find.

A pocket notebook, in which you can make notes, will also be useful. You may want to make some simple sketches too. Without a notebook it is easy to forget the details of what has been seen. Make notes about the appearance and behavior of the birds you have seen, as well as the date,

A large wooden hide or blind is often used by birdwatchers in reserves and sanctuaries.

The things you will need for watching wildfowl.

place and weather conditions.

Although wildfowl are fairly large, such details are easier to observe through binoculars. These make distant birds seem much closer and clearer. The most useful binoculars for birdwatching have the numbers 7×50 or 8×40 marked on them.

Many reserves and refuges have public hides. A hide is a structure, usually wooden, from which you can watch birds without being seen. Even so, you will have to be quiet and patient to avoid frightening the birds. Without a hide, try to be even quieter, avoid bright clothing and move slowly, making use of trees, bushes, buildings or cars as cover.

It is better and safer to go bird-watching with one or two friends or relatives, especially if they already know a lot about wildfowl. You can even join a bird club or society if you wish.

A page from a birdwatcher's notebook.

Glossary

Adapted Suited for survival in a particular habitat.

Breed To produce and rear young.

Colonies Groups of the same kind of animal or plant living close together.

Courting The behavior of male and female animals toward one another prior to mating.

Domesticated Bred and kept by humans as a pet or to provide food.

Down The soft, fine feathers that cover a bird's body and prevent loss of heat.

Drakes Male ducks.

Extinct Having died out.

Fledged Having developed a full set of feathers so as to be able to fly.

Flocks Groups of animals of the same kind, especially sheep and birds.

Habitat The natural home of an animal or plant.

Hemisphere Half of the earth, as divided by the equator.

Imprint To become emotionally attached to another creature.

Incubated Kept warm. Birds sit on their eggs to provide warmth so that the baby birds can develop.

Instinct The natural inborn response of an animal to a situation.

Magnetism The earth's magnetism is a kind of magnetic force field.

Mate The male or female of a breeding pair of animals.

Migrate To travel between different habitats at certain times of the year.

Molt To lose old feathers (or fur) and grow new ones in their place.

Navigate To find the way from one place to another.

Pesticides Chemicals used to kill pests, especially insects.

Pinioned Prevented from flying. To pinion a bird is to cut off the flight feathers.

Plankton Tiny plants and animals found in seas, lakes and rivers.

Plumage A bird's feathers.

Predators Animals that hunt and kill other animals for food.

Radar A system of radio waves used for finding and tracking moving objects.
Refuges Places where wild animals can live in safety.
Speculum A patch of colorful feathers on the wing of a bird.
Tundra The huge, treeless, Arctic region where the soil just below ground level is frozen all year.
Vegetation Plant life.

Finding Out More

The following books will help you to find out more about ducks, geese and swans.

Birds of America, by John J. Audubon. Macmillan, 1947

Wonders of Geese and Swans, by Thomas D. Fegely. Dodd, 1976.

Pond and River Birds, by John Leigh-Pemberton. Merry Thoughts, 1969.

Birdwatching on Inland Freshwaters, by Malcolm Ogilvie. Severn House, 1982.

A Field Guide to the Birds: A Completely New Guide to Birds of Eastern and Central North America, by Roger T. Peterson. 4th ed. Houghton Mifflin, 1980.

Audubon Water Bird Guide: Water, Game and Large Land Birds, by Richard H. Pough. Doubleday, 1951.

Birds of the Water, Sea and Shore, by Sandra Romashko. Winward, 1985.

Water and Shore Birds, by Walter Thiede. Merrimack, 1981.

Index

Picture Acknowledgments

All photographs by Anthony Wharton with the exception of those on pages 17, 20, 30 and 33, which are by Colin Smith. The artwork was supplied by Jackie Harland.